T0029110

Outside the Box

Like a Family

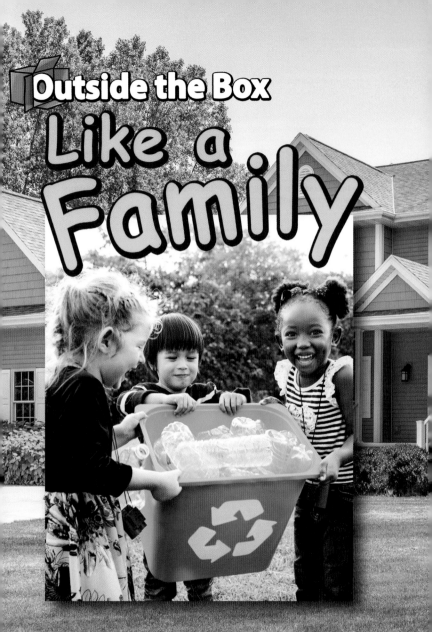

Karin Anderson

Publishing Credits

Rachelle Cracchiolo, M.S.Ed., *Publisher*
Conni Medina, M.A.Ed., *Managing Editor*
Nika Fabienke, Ed.D., *Series Developer*
June Kikuchi, *Content Director*
John Leach, *Assistant Editor*
Kevin Pham, *Graphic Designer*

TIME For Kids and the TIME For Kids logo are registered trademarks of TIME Inc.
Used under license.

Image Credits: p.11: Joseph Sohm/Shutterstock; all other images from iStock
and/or Shutterstock.

Teacher Created Materials

5301 Oceanus Drive
Huntington Beach, CA 92649-1030
http://www.tcmpub.com

ISBN 978-1-4258-4953-5

© 2018 Teacher Created Materials, Inc.

family

This is a family.
This is a big family.

This is a family.
This is a small
family.

This is a family.
I see a boy.
I see his stepmom.

This is a family.
I see a grandpa.
I see a grandma.

Friends can be like a family.
This is a **class**.

A class is like a
school family.

A **team** can be like a family.
This is a team.

A team is like a
sports family.

A **community** can be like a family. This is a group of friends.

A community is like
a neighborhood
family.

There are many
kinds of families.

Who is like a family to you?

Glossary

class

community

family

team